Y0-ABH-942

The 9 Keys To Successful Volunteer Programs

KATHLEEN BROWN FLETCHER

The Taft Group • 12300 Twinbrook Parkway
Suite 450 • Rockville, MD 20852-1607

THE NINE KEYS TO SUCCESSFUL VOLUNTEER PROGRAMS

Printed in the United States of America

90 89 88 87 86 85   6 5 4 3 2 1

Library of Congress Cataloging-in-Publication Data

Fletcher, Kathleen Brown.
  The 9 keys to successful volunteer programs.

1. Voluntarism—United States—Management.
I. Title. II. Title: Nine keys to successful
volunteer programs. III. Title: Volunteer program.
HN90.V64F56 1987   361.3'7'068   87-10179
ISBN 0-914756-28-1

The Taft Group
12300 Twinbrook Parkway, Suite 450
Rockville, MD 20852

DEDICATION

To Margery Sell, who told me I should be a Director of
Volunteers
and
To Phil Murphy, who gave me my first opportunity to be one.

Table of Contents

FOREWORD TO THE REVISED EDITION

In rereading the original edition of this book six years after writing it, I find that I am pleased by how well it has stood the test of time. I stand by everything I said when I wrote the original and have simply added material I have gathered in my consulting and training work since then. I am also pleased that many managers of volunteer programs have found the original edition a useful and practical guide in their work. I trust that the revised edition, with added emphasis on recognition and retention, will be even more helpful to those responsible for directing the work of volunteers in a wide variety of settings.

In my consulting and training work, I am continually impressed by the high-quality people I meet who have chosen the profession of volunteer program management. Some are long-time volunteers who are just entering paid work, some are young people sampling this field for the first time, some have been professional managers for many years. All have a sincere desire to manage their programs for the maximum benefit of both their volunteers and their organizations. As I state in the text of this book, to do so is often a difficult balancing act between the needs of the volunteer, the staff, and the clients of the organization. To recruit and retain workers who are not motivated by the need for a paycheck takes special sensitivity and skill, and I have found an abundance of both among the people who have taken my workshops.

The revised edition of this book, therefore, is dedicated to those thousands of men and women across this country, in Canada, and in other parts of the world who make volunteer programs work through their managerial ability and their strong sense of caring for humanity. Being a volunteer program manager may not make anyone rich, but it is one of the most satisfying jobs anyone can have. Volunteer programs make our democracy work, and good management of these programs is vital if this important segment of our society is to grow and prosper.

Kathleen Brown Fletcher
May, 1987

INTRODUCTION

This is meant to be a book of ideas, not formulas. There are no formulas that guarantee a successful volunteer program, there are only concepts and tools that those responsible for managing volunteers can apply in ways suitable to their particular programs and to their own management styles.

It has only been recently that managers of volunteer programs have begun to think of themselves as belonging to a distinct profession. As managers, they deal with many of the same issues as their counterparts in business or government—worker motivation, selection of the right person for each job, supervision, performance evaluation—and much of the literature on these management functions can be directly applied to their situations. But managers of volunteer programs have other issues to face: designing jobs that will attract volunteers, recruiting volunteers in a society where the value of volunteerism for the individual volunteer and the community is not well understood, helping professional staff work with volunteers, providing appropriate rewards for workers who don't get a paycheck, saying no to the well-meaning but unqualified people who don't understand why organizations can't use everyone who wants to volunteer. The new profession of volunteer program management must face these issues and more in order to preserve volunteerism as a vital force in America.

This book discusses nine keys that make a volunteer program work: good job design, staff commitment, well-planned recruitment, careful screening and selection, appropriate training, good supervision by staff, appropriate surveillance by the volunteer program manager, and systematic evaluation. It is based on my eight years of experience in the volunteer program management field (often learning lessons the hard way!) as well as on general management theory and practice. In writing this, I am making the assumption that every volunteer program manager will regard these ideas as tools to use in creating and managing a volunteer program that works in each individual setting. Like all tools, they are means to an end rather than ends in themselves, and their application will be tailored by the individual using them as well as by the realities of the organizational structure in which that individual works.

Kathleen M. Brown
June, 1981

ix

THE FIRST KEY:
GOOD JOB DESIGN

THE FIRST KEY: GOOD JOB DESIGN

If you ask most volunteer program managers what their primary concern is, they will say, "How do I recruit more volunteers?" Though this is a vital concern, it often reflects a lack of understanding of what must come before recruitment: 1) good job design, and 2) knowledge of the volunteer world today. Before you can successfully recruit, you must know what you're recruiting for and what types of people you want to attract.

Good job design has several distinct elements. First, ask yourself **what** you want done and give a specific, detailed answer. For instance, state that you want volunteers to type file cards for the mailing list or answer the phone and greet visitors, not that you want volunteers to help in the office. Next, ask yourself **why** it is important that this job be done; you won't be a convincing recruiter unless you yourself are convinced that the job is a vital one. Then, ask yourself why a volunteer rather than a paid staff person should do the job. Saving money on salaries isn't a good enough reason; if volunteers sense that the organization is only interested in the budget, they will also sense that they're being exploited. Your agency must have other reasons for creating volunteer opportunities, such as the desire to involve the community in your programs or to expand services available to clients. Furthermore, volunteer jobs must offer the volunteer something: a chance to learn new skills, the opportunity to be engaged in exciting human service work, social interaction, and so on. Volunteers want to feel involved, not used.

Once you've determined what you want done and why it's important for a volunteer to do it, the next step is to determine how each job fits into the organizational structure. Who will be the appropriate staff supervisor for each volunteer job? Does the appropriate person really want to supervise volunteers, or will you lose good volunteers because the wrong person is supervising them? How much staff involvement is necessary to integrate the volunteer job into the work plan for the organization? A mass mailing or a simple typing job, for instance, usually requires only instruction and monitoring by one or two staff, while training and supervising volunteer counselors involve many more staff and much more time if the job is to be responsibly done.

Finally, take a close look at each volunteer job you design to determine what the rewards will be for a volunteer who accepts that job. Does the job offer training in a skill area such as counseling, marketing, office skills, or budgeting? Does it offer social interaction and a feeling of being needed? Does it offer recognition in the community? When you actually start recruiting, you will look for people who want these rewards, e.g., re-entry women or students looking for skills training, senior citizens looking for social interaction, homemakers wanting recognition for work in the community. Knowing what each job offers to potential volunteers is of immeasurable help in planning an effective recruitment program.

A key to both job design and recruitment is the written job description (see example at end of this chapter). The form can be simple or complex as long as certain vital information is included: job title, time commitment, supervision, specific duties, and qualifications. Job descriptions can also include statements of what the job offers to the potential volunteer (training, etc.) and what the importance of the job is to the organization's purpose.

Job descriptions are also important planning tools for involving staff in the development of volunteer positions. When staff members request volunteers, you can sit down with them and fill out the blank form, helping staff specify what they want done, what qualifications volunteers must have to do the job, and what they see as the importance of the volunteer job to the work of the agency. This kind of planning is essential to a well-run volunteer program.

Good job design is a preparation for staff involvement with volunteers, for recruitment, and for effective use of volunteers in any setting. It's what you do before you do anything else, and it will make the subsequent parts of a volunteer program manager's job immeasurably easier.

ELEMENTS OF VOLUNTEER JOB DESIGN

1. The job is **needed** by the organization and its clients.

2. The job **fits** into the overall **goals and policies** of the organization.

3. The job **has specific duties.**

4. The job **fits the time frame** of potential volunteers.

5. The job **is supervised** by a specific staff member, someone who wants to work with a volunteer.

6. The job **does not take over the professional duties** of paid staff nor replace a position currently filled by a paid staff member.

7. The job **has specific policies and procedures** which are understood by both staff and volunteers.

8. The job **provides** volunteers with a **sense of satisfaction** and a feeling of belonging to the organization.

9. The job **provides learning opportunities** for volunteers.

Sample
VOLUNTEER JOB DESCRIPTION

JOB TITLE:

Phone Receptionist Volunteer

SUPERVISOR:

Office Manager

TIME COMMITMENT:

4 hours a week in regular morning or afternoon shift during office hours (Mon–Fri, 9 to 5)

DUTIES:

Answer phone in agency office, act as receptionist for office visitors, do miscellaneous office jobs as directed by staff (copying, collating, mailing, filing, running errands, typing, etc.)

QUALIFICATIONS:

Pleasant phone voice, skill in listening, ability to work independently, willingness to accept a variety of office tasks, supportive of agency philosophy, and comfortable with issues related to the work of the agency

TRAINING:

Orientation to agency with Director of Volunteers (4 hours)

On-the-job training with Office Manager and experienced volunteers (8 to 12 hours)

On-going training meeting with all office volunteers, 2 hours per month (attendance required)

IMPORTANCE OF THE JOB TO THE ORGANIZATION'S PURPOSE:

The agency receives many calls for information as well as business calls and calls from clients. The phone receptionist volunteer serves the agency's constituency by providing information and referral to callers and by forwarding business and client calls to the proper staff person.

THE SECOND KEY:
STAFF COMMITMENT

THE SECOND KEY: STAFF COMMITMENT

Though it may seem out of order to discuss staff commitment to the volunteer program before recruitment, it isn't. Getting staff involved in designing jobs and committed to making the program work are prerequisites for getting volunteers involved in the organization.

There are many misconceptions about volunteers among both professional and nonprofessional staff. For one thing, they often don't realize that volunteers aren't free: it takes time and effort to train, supervise, and evaluate them. Time and effort are also spent in providing volunteers with the appreciation and recognition they need. Volunteers must be listened to, and problems they are having or creating must be solved. All this costs the organization staff time (and supplies, telephone costs, etc.) that must be taken into account by staff and/or board members who want the organization to utilize volunteers.

Staff sometimes don't understand that volunteers need challenge, social interaction, direction, feedback, and appreciation. Some seem unaware that people who volunteer their time want something back from the organization. Thus the volunteer program manager must often spend time in awareness training for staff, e.g., helping staff recognize the needs of volunteers, the costs of a volunteer program, and the degree of commitment required. Staff members should understand what's involved **before** they agree to take on volunteers.

Sitting down with a staff member who requests a volunteer and going over the Job Description form is a good way of ascertaining whether that staff person will really support a volunteer. How does the staff person plan to supervise the volunteer? Is the time commitment asked of the volunteer reasonable? Does the job provide the volunteer with challenges and rewards or does the staff member simply want to unload some of the unpleasant parts of his job on someone else? Getting a staff member's commitment to work **with** a volunteer is an important part of creating a positive experience for both.

You should also be aware of staff members' concerns about volunteers: will they maintain confidentiality about the agency's clients, will they be reliable, will they demand excessive amounts of staff time, will they really provide a needed service? These concerns should be discussed openly and addressed in the Policies and Procedures you write for the volunteer program (see example at the end of this chapter). Discuss these Policies and Procedures at a staff meeting and make sure every staff member has a copy. Ask staff members to make suggestions for changes or additions to the Policies and Procedures, and include what they suggest unless there's something you consider unreasonable. The more input staff have into the design of the volunteer program, the more commitment they will have to its success.

Another way to promote staff commitment is to take time at each staff meeting to talk about the volunteer program. You need to bring staff up to date on new developments, ask for their feedback, and discuss any problems that have come up. Staff need to feel that the program is theirs and that they have a chance to change anything that isn't working out.

Too often volunteer programs are forced on staff by boards of directors, government regulations, or overeager program administrators who don't understand how much energy it takes to successfully involve volunteers in an organization. If you as a volunteer program manager find yourself carrying out directives from above that aren't supported by the staff who will actually be using volunteers, stop now and work for staff involvement, staff commitment, and staff appreciation of volunteers before you recruit anyone else. And, unless you can't help it, don't agree to recruit volunteers for staff members who don't really want them.

The basic question that must be answered is "Why does this organization want volunteers?" Again, there have to be reasons beyond saving salaries, especially since volunteers should not replace paid staff. Typically, organizations want to involve volunteers to extend and complement the services of paid staff, thus better serving their clients. Organizations also want to provide opportunities for community members to be involved in their work and to promote community support of the organization. If staff are convinced of the value of the volunteer program for both the agency and its clients, they are much more likely to give the necessary time and energy that will make the program work. Without this time, energy, and commitment from staff, the program is doomed to eventual, if not immediate, failure.

While program staff may worry about the effect of volunteers on themselves and on clients, executive staff may have an added worry in our litigious society: organizational liability. Though few, if any, problems have occurred, it would be a good idea to check with your insurance carrier to see whether the organization is covered should a client sue over the actions of a volunteer. Another question is whether the organization is covered should the volunteer sue for some harm alleged to have come from the volunteer job. If not, the organization may want to add to its liability coverage, though the risk factor is not great.

REASONS TO INVOLVE VOLUNTEERS IN AN ORGANIZATION

1. Offer additional services to clients

2. Serve more clients

3. Get community members involved in the organization

4. Increase community knowledge and support of the organization.

5. Relieve staff of duties that can be delegated to a volunteer

6. Provide work experience opportunities needed by youth, re-entry women, the handicapped, and those recovering from illness

Sample
POLICIES AND PROCEDURES FOR VOLUNTEERS

1. Names of agency clients and donors are to be held in strict confidence by both volunteers and staff. Inappropriate use of confidential material is sufficient grounds for termination of both salaried and volunteer staff.

2. Client records are not to be reviewed by volunteers except with permission of the Executive Director.

3. On-going training meetings are part of the volunteer job. Attendance is required unless the volunteer is excused by the Director of Volunteers.

4. When volunteers are going to be absent from their assignment, they should call the Director of Volunteers and/or their supervisor at least 24 hours in advance (except in emergencies).

5. The Director of Volunteers is the liaison between the volunteers and the agency. Volunteers should bring any problems, concerns, or suggestions to the Director of Volunteers and should let him/her know if they would like a change in assignment.

6. Volunteers are required to sign in and out when they work in the office. Volunteers who do not report to the office are required to turn in their hours monthly to the Director of Volunteers.

7. Volunteer performance will be formally evaluated by the Director of Volunteers with input from other staff every six months. Volunteers will also be asked to evaluate their own performance at that time.

8. Volunteers will be asked for an evaluation of the volunteer program periodically and also upon their leaving the program. Comments and suggestions are welcome at other times as well.

THE THIRD KEY:
WELL-PLANNED RECRUITMENT

THE THIRD KEY: WELL-PLANNED RECRUITMENT

Americans have always volunteered in great numbers: in community service, politics, religious causes, health care, schools, youth activities, and numerous other arenas. They volunteer in many different capacities: as service club members, fund raisers, board members, youth group leaders, political organizers, peer counselors, museum docents, and so on. There is no shortage of volunteers in America, but there is a lack of knowledge of how to find them, appeal to them, and put them to work.

Potential volunteers are choosy these days; they want to work in jobs where they can give the amount of time they have available and gain real satisfaction. Some have specific goals, such as students looking for internship credit, re-entry women looking for training and job experience, or newcomers looking for involvement in the community. Housewives, the traditional source of volunteers, are available in fewer and fewer numbers, but they're still out there and still become involved in organizations they care about. In addition, there are new groups to draw from: retired people wanting to stay active, singles seeking social contacts, people serving alternative sentences (court referral programs), young people wanting to build references, people in transition from one career or life phase to another. Service clubs and churches still provide willing hands, and self-help groups such as co-ops and neighborhood associations willingly give time for their mutual good. It may be a different volunteer world today, but it's still a strong one.

A special challenge in today's world is how to involve employed people. It can be done, but it takes tailoring the job to fit the individual's schedule. Professionals (lawyers, doctors, accountants, etc.) will often volunteer in their area of expertise for special projects or occasional service to nonprofit groups. Many corporations encourage employees (particularly those at high levels of management) to donate time to community groups as board members, financial planners, and so on. Some corporations have active employee volunteer programs at the factory or office worker level. And some working people simply want to do more than they do on the job; they want enrichment or new skills, and they'll volunteer if the job fits into their nonwork time.

There are other sources of volunteers: people recovering from disease, addiction, or emotional trauma (sometimes called Transitional Volunteer Programs), people caught up in enthusiasm for a cause (political, environmental, social), parents in their children's activities, nonparent adults wanting contact with children, people wishing to promote a particular interest or hobby (such as the arts), former clients of an agency who wish to give what they once received. The list is probably endless; the important thing is to figure out which groups your organization's volunteer jobs would appeal to and how best to reach those groups.

Determining a target group is thus the next step in preparing to recruit volunteers. Usually the recruitment methods to choose will logically follow this determination. For instance, if you decide you want to recruit retired people to fill classroom aide jobs, you'll think about ways to reach retired people: senior citizen group newsletters, retirement center bulletin boards, speaking engagements at clubs for seniors, distribution of brochures in retirement communities.

You might also want to write recruitment material and ask parents to distribute it to retired neighbors or grandparents. If you make it clear that you specifically want retired people to be involved in the school system because of the experience, expertise, and grandparental love they can offer, you should get a much better response than with a general appeal. Deciding on a target group, determining what members of that group are likely to be seeking, and showing through your recruitment materials how your job can provide what they want are common sense, effective approaches to recruitment.

Here are some other examples of this approach. If you have a responsible office job to fill, it's likely to appeal to people preparing for entry or re-entry into the job market. You would probably want to publicize the job in the local newspaper, and you could also try community college bulletin boards, business schools, supermarket or laundromat bulletin boards, and career counseling centers. You might also want to place a paid ad in the Help Wanted section. You would emphasize the value of volunteer work in establishing an employment record through references, resume additions, and skills practice. Of course, your job would truly have to offer these things to volunteers; if you want only envelope stuffers, choose target groups looking not for job skills but for social interaction. Plan a mailing party in a senior citizens' home, or get a service-oriented singles or youth group to help. If you want professional consultation, call the Public Relations Department of a local business or the president of a professional organization and emphasize both the need of your organization and the public relations value of helping you.

If all of this sounds like marketing, it is—and those in volunteer program management must make good use of marketing techniques if volunteer work is to compete with all the other ways people can spend their free time. Knowing who your volunteer jobs would appeal to and why, then using that information in deciding where to recruit and which methods to use, are essential. This is marketing, but it's not manipulation; you really do have something to offer potential volunteers, and your recruitment materials should state your case honestly and directly. Anything less than a well-thought-out, well-presented recruitment campaign does a disservice to both your organization and the potential volunteers who would benefit from working with you.

Now some words about recruitment techniques. There are many to choose from, and you will want to use as many as are appropriate. Newspapers, club or business newsletters, church bulletins, posters, brochures, and radio and TV public service announcements can all be used to reach interested people. Copy for newspapers, newsletters, or bulletins should include: 1) the title, duties, and time commitment of the job you're filling; 2) a sentence or two about what your organization does; 3) a statement about what kind of training will be provided; and 4) a name and phone number to call for further information. (See example at the end of this chapter.) Posters and brochures should be as eye-catching and professional as possible. If you, the volunteer program manager, aren't artistically inclined, see if you can recruit someone who is from a local school or business, or see if you can get a donation to pay for the services of a graphic artist. As for public service announcements, call your local radio and TV stations to find out what their policies are, then write your material to fit the policies. When any of the above methods bring results, it's also important public relations to thank the newspaper, radio station, or other group which publicized your volunteer opportunity.

Information and orientation meetings, courses, speaking engagements, and one-to-one appeals are effective recruitment techniques because of their direct, personal nature. You can, for instance, invite potential volunteers to a meeting in which you present your organization and the volunteer opportunities you offer. Perhaps you can show a slide presentation or have a staff member speak; you can also ask present volunteers to share their experiences with the potential volunteers who attend. If you use written job descriptions, you can distribute them and have people fill out an information form or application indicating which job they'd like to be interviewed for. Holding this meeting is a second step, of course; the first is to publicize the meeting through newspapers, bulletins, radio, TV, and posters. Good publicity and good planning for the meeting itself are essential.

Another way to recruit volunteers is to offer a course to the public on what your organization does. Besides serving as the first step in training new volunteers, a course also provides a significant service to the community **and** has public relations value for the organization even if some of the course participants don't become volunteers. Examples of this type of course are "Crisis Intervention and Suicide Prevention" sponsored by the Suicide Prevention Center, "Hospice Care for the Terminally Ill" sponsored by a hospice program, "Child Abuse Prevention" sponsored by the Family Service Agency, and "Youth, Drugs, and Alcohol" sponsored by an alcohol and drug treatment center. It's reasonable and usually necessary to charge a fee for courses like these since they involve much staff time in planning, preparation, and delivery. If done properly, they give participants useful information and serve as pretraining sessions for potential volunteers. Throughout the course, you can talk about your volunteer program, and at the last session those who are interested can indicate that they'd like an interview with you. As with the information/orientation meetings, one key to the success of using courses as recruitment tools is good publicity beforehand.

Many organizations find that speaking engagements at clubs,

churches, and schools are effective for volunteer recruitment as well as for public relations and fund raising. You can create a Speakers Bureau of staff and volunteers, then contact groups that use speakers and offer your presentation. You need people who are comfortable speaking to groups and a well-thought-out, personalized presentation. Sometimes former clients of the organization make very effective speakers. However, a poor presentation by anyone on your behalf can cause more harm than good, so exercise caution in creating a public speaking program. Done well, it can be a very effective use of your time and energy.

One-to-one recruitment of potential volunteers by present volunteers is probably the best method anyone could use. If your present volunteers are involved and excited, they will approach their friends with the kind of sincere persuasive techniques that no carefully planned recruitment drive can duplicate. Developing and managing a good volunteer program lead to satisfied volunteers, and they are your most effective recruiters. If your program gives them the rewards they're seeking, they'll be very likely to respond to an appeal from you to recruit more volunteers, and those they recruit will be likely to respond favorably.

There are also indirect methods of recruitment that can be effective. The local Volunteer Center interviews many potential volunteers and can steer those who might be interested in your jobs toward your organization. Keeping the Volunteer Center informed of your needs is thus important. Also, a good working relationship with other directors of volunteers in your community can help; if they interview someone who's wrong for them and right for you, they can send that person your way. Taking part in Community Service Days or Volunteer Fairs can also help your program grow.

Now a very important recruitment tool that's often overlooked: a year-round public relations program. The more favorable an impression people have of your organization's work, the more likely they are to respond eventually to a recruitment appeal. Sometimes people become interested in what you're doing months or years before they have the time or inclination to volunteer for you. So keeping your work known through newspaper articles, speaking engagements, courses, radio and TV informational spots, brochures, slide presentations, and other methods is crucial to maintaining the long-term support you need from the community and instrumental in getting you the volunteers you want.

To summarize, effective recruitment follows good job design and solid staff commitment. Many recruitment methods can be used, but for maximum results they should be directed to specific target groups who would be interested in specific jobs, and should emphasize what those jobs offer to these groups. A year-round public relations program is a valuable adjunct to any successful recruitment drive.

And now, if you've done your recruitment well, you have some people who have responded to your appeal and you're ready for the next step: screening and selection of those who will be your new volunteers.

WHO VOLUNTEERS AND WHY

1. Homemakers seeking community involvement

2. Students seeking experience and/or credit

3. Professionals in their area of expertise

4. People in transition from one career or life phase to another

5. Employees of corporations with active programs

6. Retired people wishing to stay active

7. Working people seeking enrichment or new skills

8. People recovering from disease, addiction, or emotional trauma

9. People caught up in enthusiasm for a cause

10. Parents in their children's activities

11. People with particular interests or hobbies, e.g., the arts

12. People in self-help groups, e.g., co-ops, neighborhood associations

13. Singles seeking social contacts

14. Agency clients or former clients

15. People new to the community

16. People serving alternative sentences (court referral programs)

METHODS TO RECRUIT VOLUNTEERS

1. Newspapers
2. Information meetings/orientation meetings
3. Bulletins and newsletters
4. Courses
5. Speaking engagements
6. One-to-one recruitment
7. Slides, films, etc.
8. Brochures
9. Posters
10. Volunteer Centers
11. Community Service Days
12. Radio and TV spots
13. Year-round public relations program

Sample
JOB ANNOUNCEMENT—MEDIA RELEASE

TO: **DAILY NEWS**

FROM: XYZ Agency
111 Main Street
City, State   Zip
555-5555
Mary Jones, Director of Volunteers

FOR IMMEDIATE RELEASE   **January 2, 1987**

VOLUNTEER TYPIST NEEDED

XYZ Agency needs a person with good typing skills to volunteer four hours a week in the office to type file cards and keep the mailing list up to date. XYZ Agency is a treatment center for alcoholics serving the entire county. Orientation to XYZ's program and training for the job will be provided. Call Mary Jones at 555-5555 for further information.

Sample
RADIO SPOT

TO: **Station KALL**

FROM: People Service Center
        11 Main Street
        City, State   Zip
        999-9999
        John Smith, Director of Volunteers

30-Second Spot

Training classes for the People Support Hotline will be held Friday and Saturday at the People Services Center.

Volunteers assisted by professional counselors operate a 24-hour crisis hotline dealing with problems such as anxiety and depression, child abuse, alcohol and drug abuse.

Training sessions will be held Friday from noon to 5 PM and Saturday from 9 AM to 4 PM. Call the Center at 999-9999 for further information.

ACTIVITY FLYER

HOSPICE TRAINING
"INTRODUCTION TO HOSPICE CARE"

A 7-week course sponsored by Hospice of This City

Wednesday evenings, September 17 to October 29, 1987
Hospice office: 90 Main Street, (This City)
7:30 to 10:00 PM

- For those interested in learning about the hospice philosophy and methods of care for the terminally ill

and

- For those interested in doing volunteer work with hospice patients

The course subjects will include:

- Supportive care for the terminally ill at home or in health care facilities

- The disease process of cancer

- The family dynamics in terminal illness

- Psychological and spiritual support for patients and families

- The effects of a death on surviving family members

- The impact of the hospice movement on the health care system

Course faculty will include staff members from the Hospice of (This City) and special guest speakers
(list them, if known, with their affiliations)

Enrollment limited to twenty-five   Fee: $35.00

For further information and registration procedures, call
222-2222

THE FOURTH KEY:
CAREFUL SCREENING AND SELECTION

THE FOURTH KEY: CAREFUL SCREENING AND SELECTION

One of the hardest parts of the volunteer program manager's job is selecting appropriate volunteers and screening out those who are inappropriate for the jobs being filled. One reason for this is the difficulty of recruiting volunteers in the first place; you can be so grateful that someone wants to work with you that you overlook his or her lack of qualifications or inappropriate motivation. Another reason is the lack of professional interviewing skills found among many volunteer program managers coupled with the reticence to ask probing questions. A third reason is the lack of patience on the part of the organization and the desire to please on the part of the volunteer program manager; together these can bring about a hasty screening and selection process that backfires later as inappropriate volunteers cause problems for staff and/or clients.

Screening out inappropriate volunteers before you even interview them is the first step in a careful selection process. If you design and define your volunteer jobs well, people can screen themselves out by simply looking at a job description and realizing they don't have either the time or the qualifications necessary for the job. Of course, you may want to be flexible to accommodate someone you really want to volunteer for you, but remember that the needs of the organization and the people it serves come before the needs of the potential volunteer. If in your recruitment drives you accurately depict what the volunteer can expect to get from the job, those who want something else can look elsewhere. You will save yourself time and energy as well as disappointment on the part of potential volunteers if you define your jobs well enough so that people can screen themselves out if the job doesn't fit them. You can also help such people find a job that does fit by referring them to the Volunteer Bureau or another agency in the community that you think might have what they want.

Now, about interviewing those who are left, those who have responded to your recruitment appeal and have not screened themselves out. A whole book could be written about interviewing, but here are a few suggestions for successful interviews. First, sit down beforehand and make a list of the things you really need to know about the potential volunteer. If, for instance, you are interviewing for counselors in a drug treatment center, you may really need to know if the volunteer has ever had a drug problem or experience with a close friend or family member who has. The same is true for child abuse, suicide prevention, grief counseling, and other sensitive areas. Sometimes a simple "Why are you interested in this work?" will elicit the information you want, but if not, you may need to ask. Of course, many jobs aren't as sensitive as counseling, and for them you may not have to ask such probing questions. But if you're interviewing people who will work with your organization's clients, you owe it to everyone, including the potential volunteers, to find out what kind of personal involvement they've had with the problems your organization addresses. Just because people have had personal experience doesn't disqualify them; it may, in fact, make them more sensitive to your clients. But the important thing to determine is whether they have worked through and overcome their drug problem, suicidal tendencies, or grief; if they haven't, they may want to use your volunteer job as therapy for themselves rather than to help your clients. In such cases, volunteer program managers and other staff often find themselves trying to be therapists for volunteers, and everyone is shortchanged, especially the clients who need counseling.

The depth and nature of the questions you ask will vary with your organization and type of volunteer jobs, but you will almost always want to ask why people are interested and what they would like to get from their work for your organization. If they don't know, that's all right; the intuition that this is something they'd like to do is perfectly acceptable in many cases. But if they want something you know you can't offer, you can tell them so and give them some alternate suggestions. You may also want to find out what they feel they have to offer to your program and what new skills or understandings they would like to develop. You may want to find out about their hobbies and interests and perhaps about their family and employment. Don't get too personal, though, unless the answer to a particular question is relevant to the potential volunteer's appropriateness for your program. This would violate Equal Employment Opportunity regulations which, although they don't legally apply to volunteer work, should still be respected by those who interview applicants for volunteer positions.

A good way to start an interview is to refer to an information form that the volunteer has previously filled out. There is almost always something interesting you can pick up on to break the ice, such as an unusual hobby, relevant work or volunteer experience, something common to you and the volunteer (you went to the same college?), or a statement that warrants further explanation. Starting the interview by showing interest in information the volunteer has put on the form usually gets things going in a smooth and friendly manner. An information form also gives you a written document to put on file and/or pass on to any other staff member who will interview the potential volunteer.

Now some standard interviewing advice: 1) Make the interviewee comfortable, offer coffee or tea, give him or her your full attention, don't answer calls or get distracted by anything else that's going on in the office; 2) Ask open questions like "What kinds of counseling experience have you had?" rather than questions requiring only a yes or no answer; 3) Give the interviewee time to ask you questions about the organization or the specific job as well as plenty of time to answer your questions; 4) Ask your questions in a friendly, nonthreatening way so you don't put the interviewee on the defensive; 5) Don't rush to cover silences since the most useful information often comes after the interviewee ponders his or her answer for a while; 6) Use the interview as a mutual selection process. Don't assume beforehand that the volunteer definitely wants the job or that you definitely want the volunteer; let the interview help clarify these questions.

A further piece of advice is to cultivate patience. Volunteer program managers are sometimes so enthusiastic about their organization or so desperate for volunteers that they oversell during an interview, or they overlook potentially troubling issues they should be pursuing. Remember that you're not doing your organization any favor by selecting inappropriate volunteers. If the right volunteer doesn't come along immediately, have faith and wait rather than rush someone who's inappropriate into the position just to have it filled. If there's pressure from staff, you may have to stand up for the principle of matching the person to the job. And if the right person never comes, it may be that the job is poorly designed. In that case, help staff change their expectations, write a new job description, and start over again!

Another suggestion about interviewing is to trust your intuition. Be sensitive to that feeling in your stomach that "something is wrong here." Perhaps the person's words don't fit his or her manner; perhaps you feel the person isn't right for the job even though you can't put your finger on the reason. If you feel comfortable in doing so, you can share your intuition with the interviewee in a nonthreatening manner; for instance, you can say something like "I'm getting the feeling that you really want a job that offers more interaction with staff and clients." This can lead to a discussion that clarifies potential problems for both interviewer and interviewee. At any rate, don't dismiss your "gut" feelings; they're often the best thing you have going for you in selecting volunteers.

Sometimes during an interview (or even before) you will know immediately that the potential volunteer is inappropriate and you will find yourself having to say "no, thank you" in the kindest way possible. In such situations, you can often steer the person toward another volunteer job in your agency or toward a different kind of volunteer job with another agency in your area. If the person hasn't been to the local voluntary action center, you can explain that that organization helps match volunteers with requests from agencies and suggest that the person contact the Volunteer Center for an interview.

When you say "No" to a potential volunteer, you will want to be as honest as you can without hurting the person's feelings. Give your reasons without implying that the person is innately inadequate. For instance, if you tell people that they haven't had enough background or training for the job, you have given an objective fact that should be less painful than a subjective rejection. Sometimes your reason can be valuable feedback to the volunteer and can help the two of you find a better placement. For instance, you might have to tell a person with a heavy foreign accent that you can't use him or her as a phone volunteer but that there are plenty of jobs where the accent would not be an impediment. If a potential volunteer tries to argue with your decision, you will need to stand firmly by your judgment, but you can do so without becoming angry or rejecting the person as an individual. Saying "no" is difficult, and you will have to use all your tact and sensitivity to do it well. But remember that your job is to make your program work, and part of that job is to use your professional judgment in choosing the right volunteers.

And finally, after you've chosen volunteers you think are appropriate, let the staff people who are actually going to be working with the volunteers interview them and make the final decision. (The volunteers should know about this two-step interviewing process from the beginning so they don't learn at the end of the interview with you that they now have to talk to someone else.) It's important that staff members who will supervise volunteers have the opportunity to say "no, thank you" if they don't think a particular volunteer is right for the job. Usually the volunteer will have sensed a conflict, too, and will be happy to be assigned elsewhere. Remember that your program will only work if staff as well as potential volunteers are satisfied with and involved in the selection process.

QUESTIONS YOU MAY WANT TO ASK POTENTIAL VOLUNTEERS

1. Why are you interested in this job?

2. What personal experience have you had with the agency's area of specialization (drug abuse, child care, handicapped, etc.)? How were your experiences resolved?

3. What would you like to get from this volunteer job?

4. What do you feel you can contribute to the agency's work?

5. What are your hobbies and interests?

6. Can you make a commitment of six months or a year to the volunteer job?

7. What would you like to know about the agency, its clients, and the volunteer job itself?

8. How does the volunteer job fit in with your present life situation?

TIPS ON INTERVIEWING POTENTIAL VOLUNTEERS

1. Have the potential volunteer fill out an information form and use it as a conversation starter.

2. Make the interviewee comfortable; offer coffee or tea, give him/her your full attention; don't answer calls or get distracted by other things going on in the office.

3. Ask open questions, not questions that can be answered "yes" or "no."

4. Give the interviewee time to ask you questions about your organization and the volunteer job.

5. Give time for the interviewee to fully answer your questions; don't rush to cover silences.

6. Use the interview as a mutual selection process, as a dialogue between you and the interviewee in which you both get a sense of whether the job is right for this person.

7. Use your intuition; if something feels wrong, it probably is.

8. Be patient; don't try to sell the job to the wrong volunteer.

9. Let staff who will supervise the volunteer help make the final decision.

Sample
VOLUNTEER INFORMATION FORM

Name_____M (   ) F (   )

Address_____City_____Zip_____

Home Phone_____Work Phone_____

What type of volunteer work are you interested in?_____

_____

When are you available? Days_____Hours_____

Background Information

Education_____

_____

Paid Work Experience_____

_____

Volunteer Work Experience_____

_____

Special Interests or Hobbies_____

_____

Reasons for seeking volunteer work with this organization:___

_____

_____

_____

_____

_____

THE FIFTH KEY:
APPROPRIATE TRAINING

THE FIFTH KEY: APPROPRIATE TRAINING

Once volunteers have been recruited, screened, and selected, they must be trained for their jobs. The training can be short or lengthy, simple or complex, depending on what the job requires. But training is vital; volunteers have the **right** to be trained for whatever they are asked to do.

Volunteer training should include orientation to the organization, instruction in the specific job, supervised on-the-job training as the volunteer begins work, and on-going training as the volunteer continues. For complex, sensitive jobs such as phone counseling or working with handicapped children, the training will be extensive; for simpler jobs such as office work, an orientation plus instruction in the specific duties may suffice. The important things are that the training be appropriate to the job and that the volunteer be given enough information and practice to be able to do the job well.

An explanation of the work of your organization, the types of clients it serves, the structure of the organization, its funding sources, and its role in the community can be covered in a presentation by staff, supplemented by a handbook for volunteers. Sometimes the new volunteer will have attended an orientation meeting before being selected as a volunteer, but it's important to cover essential areas again. Creating a handbook with the history of the organization, a staff list and organizational chart, funding sources, client profiles, policies and procedures for volunteers, and other relevant information is a good way to make sure new volunteers have the background information you feel they need. On their first day, you will also want to give them a tour of your office and/or facility and introduce them to the staff who are present.

Some jobs will require extensive training in a classroom-like setting before the volunteer begins. The training is usually extended over a period of time; for instance, a training course might consist of one three-hour session per week for eight weeks. Whatever the time frame, the training should provide a mixture of **informational** and **experiential** methods. One useful format for a once-a-week session (three hours or so) is one and one-half hours of lecture or other informational presentation, followed by a short break, followed by one and one-half hours of role play or other experiential exercise. In all sessions, time should be allowed for questions, discussion, and reactions to the experiences.

For the **informational** part of the training, you need to decide what subject areas you want to cover and how they should be presented to your trainees. For instance, a class on suicide prevention for hotline counselors might include presentations on the causes of suicide, the responsibilities and limitations of suicide prevention, the effect of various drugs on the body, the relationship of alcoholism to suicide, how to deal with suicidal callers, and where to refer callers for further help. Once the subjects have been determined, you'll need to decide who should present them to the trainees. You may have enough expertise on your staff, or you may want to call on outside resources. You may also find films, videotapes, or slide shows that present the information you want to get across.

Whether you have staff or outside presenters, you have a choice of methods: 1) lecture with question and answer period; 2) panel discussion using several experts; 3) observation and demonstration with staff playing the roles of volunteer and client; 4) assigned readings (usually in the form of handouts); 5) films or other media presentations followed by discussion. Using a variety of these methods will make the informational presentations more interesting. Choosing good speakers for lectures and panel discussions is also very important. Even the most vital and interesting topic can be boring if you've selected the wrong speaker!

For best results in training, this informational component should be balanced with an **experiential** component, that is, with exercises in which people can clarify their attitudes, learn to empathize with the clients they will be serving, and practice doing the actual work in a safe setting. For attitude clarification, questionnaires (such as one on attitudes toward teenage sexuality used in a training program for volunteers in a teen health center) are useful since people can learn about themselves through their answers. Simulation experiences (such as one used in a recent hospice training which takes people through the losses they would experience as death approaches) can help people relate to your clients with empathy. Role play experiences, such as talking to a caller in crisis (followed by a critique from the trainee group), give people practice and feedback that's invaluable in learning to do the job. Staff who are monitoring these experiential exercises can also pick out potential problems with new volunteers and can either provide extra training or recommend that the volunteer be counseled out of the job.

A word of caution is in order, however. Experiential exercises can be very powerful, especially if they awaken latent fears or unresolved conflicts in trainees. Always follow experiential exercises with a debriefing and feedback session, and personally follow up on anyone who seems to be in pain or unduly disturbed by the exercise. In other words, be prepared to handle **anything** that comes up in response to an experiential exercise.

Besides giving both information and experience to new volunteers, extended training helps build teamwork among volunteers and staff and allows further screening and selection before volunteers actually begin their new work. Sometimes volunteers will realize that the job isn't for them and sometimes, as previously mentioned, staff will decide that a volunteer isn't appropriate. Those who complete the training and remain committed to volunteering will not only be prepared for the work but will also have "passed the test" and be ready to become part of the volunteer/staff team that serves your clients.

Extended training courses should always be evaluated by both trainees and staff. This can be done with a checklist or rating form, several essay questions, a group discussion, or a combination of several methods. However you do it, you will want to look seriously at the constructive criticism and incorporate suggested changes into your next training.

Once formal orientation and training, short or lengthy, have been completed, volunteers need on-the-job training supervised by staff or experienced volunteers until they feel comfortable in their new jobs. For instance, new phone volunteers can work with experienced ones for two shifts, or classroom aides can observe and be observed by the teacher for a few sessions before they take a group off to one corner and work with them alone. If the job is simple (e.g., typing donation acknowledgments on a standard form), the on-the-job training will be short; if it's more complex, longer apprenticeship will be required. At the end of this period, the volunteers should feel ready to tackle the job on their own.

Involving experienced volunteers in the training of new volunteers can be very beneficial to your program. Not only do new relationships develop, but experienced volunteers feel needed and appreciated for their skill. Experienced volunteers can help you plan your upcoming training events. They can also help with physical set-up for training sessions and give presentations about their work to those being trained. Such involvement in training often strengthens the ties of experienced volunteers to the organization as well as encourages them to review material they may have forgotten.

Training should not end with initial sessions; on-going training is equally important. Decide how often you think on-going training should occur and then make it a part of the volunteer job to attend on-going training sessions. Write it into the job description and make sure anyone you interview understands its importance. Too often volunteer program managers complain that volunteers don't attend monthly meetings or other on-going training sessions. This problem can often be overcome by making it clear to volunteers from the beginning that on-going training is an essential part of the volunteer job and that all volunteers are expected to attend. Of course, if meetings are too frequent, boring, irrelevant, or scheduled at inconvenient times, it's not the volunteers' fault, and the volunteer program manager needs to find out why people aren't attending and make necessary adjustments.

Subjects for on-going training can be suggested by both volunteers and staff. Outside speakers can present new material, films can be shown, case studies can be discussed, or volunteers can simply share their experiences and get suggestions and support from their peers. On-going training, like initial training, builds teamwork and helps staff spot potential problems. It also gives volunteers a chance to make suggestions or air complaints about the work.

On-going training can take many forms (e.g., two-hour meetings once a month or all-day workshops every four months), but common sense suggests there should be just enough training to accomplish your goals without overburdening the volunteers or the staff. Expecting volunteers to attend a three-hour meeting every week, for instance, is usually unrealistic, but not having them meet at all robs them of valuable growth experiences and peer relationships, and robs you of the chance to get important information on how well the volunteers are doing their jobs. On-going training is **important,** and if your volunteers aren't attending the sessions you set up, ask them to tell you what's wrong, and make whatever changes (in time, content, frequency, etc.) are needed.

Since people learn with a combination of factual information and experience, on-going training, like initial training, should provide both. Vary your training methods among lecture, discussion, audio-visual, role play, case study, simulation, etc. Allow time for people to become truly involved through question and answer sessions, small group discussion, problem solving exercises, individual writing, and debriefing after role plays. Remember that people **want** to learn, and it's the trainer's responsibility to provide them with materials and methods by which they can learn.

To receive training in a particular area of knowledge or skill is one of the reasons why many people want to do volunteer work. It's something volunteer program managers can offer to potential volunteers, and, if done well, it can be a powerful motivator for both new and experienced volunteers. If you need help in planning for this vital area, see if you can get it from a local community college, a corporate training department, or a professional training company. It's too important an area to be carelessly done. Appropriate, high-quality training is indeed a key to the success of any volunteer program.

TRAINING AGENDA FOR VOLUNTEERS

A. Basic information about your organization and its services

    1. Organizational structure and history
    2. Staff pattern
    3. Clients served
    4. Types of services offered
    5. Funding
    6. Where your organization fits into the community

B. Information about the specific job

    1. Policies regarding volunteers in your organization
    2. Procedures for the specific job
    3. Where the job fits into the organization's work
    4. What staff expect of volunteers

C. Experience with the job

    1. Role plays and simulations as part of the training course
    2. On-the-job training by experienced volunteers and/or staff
    3. On-going training as needed

D. Methods of imparting information

    1. Lecture
    2. Panel discussion
    3. Films, slides, tapes
    4. Reading assignments

E. Methods of group participation

    1. Facilitated discussion
    2. Questions and answers
    3. Let group set topic and/or agenda
    4. Have experienced volunteers do parts of the training

F. Experiential exercises

    1. Role play
    2. Simulation

3. Group problem solving
4. Individual work with materials provided
5. Questionnaires (on attitudes, for example)
6. Written assignments

SAMPLE
TRAINING COURSE EVALUATION FOR COMMUNITY HOTLINE COUNSELOR TRAINING

1. Were you satisfied with the amount of information given on the following subjects?

	Yes	No
History and philosophy of the organization		
Duties of hotline counselors		
Types of calls received		
Principles of crisis intervention		
Resources in the community		

Comments:

2. Were you satisfied with the following experiential exercises?

	Yes	No
Role plays		
Case discussions		
Crisis simulation exercises		
Written homework assignments		

Comments:

3. What additional subjects would have been helpful?

_____

4. Can you suggest changes in the scheduling or physical arrangements of the training?

_____

5. Is there anything you would delete from the training as you experienced it?

_____

PLEASE MAKE ANY FURTHER COMMENTS OR SUGGESTIONS ON THE BACK OF THIS PAGE.

THANK YOU FOR YOUR PARTICIPATION!

THE SIXTH KEY:
GOOD SUPERVISION BY STAFF

THE SIXTH KEY: GOOD SUPERVISION BY STAFF

Every person who works in an organization, whether paid or not, deserves to be well supervised. Too often volunteers are recruited, selected, and trained, then left on their own to do the work. Not only can this lead to problems for both clients and staff, it also tells volunteers that their work is not important enough to merit attention. That's an excellent way to lose good volunteers!

The first ingredient for good supervision is the designation of a specific staff person to whom the volunteer is responsible. This should be built into the job description and, as previously mentioned, the supervisor should be someone who *wants* to work with a volunteer, someone who understands and accepts the need to spend time and energy to make the volunteer situation work. Sometimes the director of volunteers can also be the supervisor of individual volunteers, but this usually isn't the case. Unless a volunteer works directly for you, it's better that someone else be the supervisor (office manager for office volunteers, social worker for counseling volunteers, teacher for classroom volunteers, and so on).

If the volunteer program is to work well, you must impress on staff how important good supervision is, and you must provide training and consulting to those staff members who take on the role of supervisor. In order to do this, you need to understand what constitutes good supervision. This chapter will outline the important elements of supervision as they relate to staff who work with volunteers.

Good supervision of volunteers includes:
- giving complete instructions and being available for questions;
- making sure expectations are clear;
- showing appreciation;
- confronting inappropriate behavior; and
- being flexible in meeting the volunteers' needs.

Lack of one or more of these elements is often the downfall of a volunteer work situation.

Instruction is part of initial training but goes beyond that. Volunteers need to be able to ask someone for directions, to check with someone about whether they're doing something right. Since volunteers usually spend only a few hours per week at their volunteer jobs, they may forget specific instructions from week to week until they've been on the job for a month or two. And since they're not around much, they may not hear about new developments or changes in the organization. The supervisor needs to be readily available to the volunteer and to remember to pass on anything of importance about the organization (or the client a volunteer is working with) to the volunteer. Being available and giving clear direction is especially important for a supervisor working with a volunteer who sees clients, since no amount of initial training can prepare volunteers for every client situation they will encounter. They need to talk regularly with their supervisor about the progress of their cases and ask questions about how they're handling each new thing that comes up.

Clear expectations on the part of both volunteer and staff supervisor are another important ingredient of a good work situation. A supervisor should know why the volunteer is there—whether that person wants training, job experience, social contacts, or whatever—and should try to meet those expectations if they are realistic. If not, it may be that the volunteer is wrong for the job or the supervisor is wrong for that volunteer. The volunteer should know what the supervisor expects as well, and should be given the chance to make suggestions if those expectations seem unreasonable given the amount of time or training the volunteer has. Getting expectations out on the table and then working out any misunderstandings are crucial steps in making a volunteer job situation work. Too often the expectations of staff and/or volunteer are not met, but neither says anything and the situation simmers until the volunteer burns out or the staff member refuses to work with volunteers any longer.

Showing appreciation is one of the easiest yet most often overlooked ingredients of good supervision (of paid or unpaid staff!). Saying "thank you" to the volunteers when they leave for the day, praising them for a job well done, mentioning their work to other staff, telling the Director of Volunteers what a good job they're doing—all these take little time and effort but bring important results. Volunteers who feel appreciated give more and continue to be positive voices in the organization and the community; volunteers who feel unappreciated often go away mad. Whether the agency has a formal recognition program or not (pins, certificates, dinners, awards, etc.), appreciation from the volunteer's direct supervisor is vital.

Next, **confrontation**—often the hardest thing for staff to do with volunteers. Because volunteers aren't being paid, many staff assume you can't tell them they're not doing a good job. But that's simply not true; as a matter of fact, it's the right of every volunteer to receive **constructive** feedback that will help improve performance. If volunteers are continuously late and this inconveniences the staff, the supervisor can ask them to be on time. If their work is sloppy, the supervisor can tactfully ask them to be neater. If they're not doing well with a client, the supervisor needs to meet with them and make suggestions. Usually volunteers will welcome this kind of constructive confrontation since they almost always sense a problem even if it hasn't been expressed. Doing nothing about work that isn't satisfactory may say to the volunteer that the work isn't important enough for staff to care about its quality. This, like poor supervision in general, can cause the loss of volunteers who would do an excellent job if they were given a little help and encouragement. Confronting inappropriate behavior in a volunteer says "I care about you, your work, and our organization," and volunteers need to hear that message.

Being **flexible** simply addresses the fact that volunteer work is usually not the first or second priority in people's lives. Even very responsible individuals put family and paid work before volunteer work, and other activities may intrude as well. Thus, while expecting volunteers to be reliable and responsible, staff must expect that some things will interfere—a sick child or a special meeting called by the volunteer's employer, for instance. If volunteers understand the importance of their work and feel needed, they will show up unless a serious family or work commitment intervenes. However, if they are made to feel guilty for sometimes putting other things first, they will probably just leave the organization. By the way, the need to be flexible and expect that volunteers will not always be able to fulfill their commitments is one very good reason why volunteers should supplement, not supplant, paid staff.

As stated before, the volunteer program manager plays an important role in staff supervision of volunteers. Volunteer program managers should encourage staff to make their expectations clear to volunteers, to be available when volunteers need direction or feedback, to show appreciation to volunteers, to confront volunteers constructively when their performance isn't what it should be, and to be flexible in meeting volunteers' needs. The volunteer program manager's responsibility is to support staff as they take on the role of supervisor of the volunteers who work for them.

THE SEVENTH KEY:
APPROPRIATE SURVEILLANCE

THE SEVENTH KEY:
APPROPRIATE SURVEILLANCE

Surveillance may seem like a strange word to use in the context of volunteer program management, but it's meant to convey the idea of watching over the volunteer program once it's in motion. As mentioned in the last section, directors of volunteers do not usually act as supervisors of volunteers; instead, they design jobs with input from staff, then recruit, screen, select, orient, and train or set up training for volunteers. Once a volunteer has been trained and assigned, the volunteer program manager's role changes to that of keeping track of each volunteer and his or her work situation, intervening in any volunteer/staff situation that isn't working, providing on-going training, keeping records and statistics, providing recognition for volunteers, evaluating the volunteers' performance and the volunteer program in general, writing and speaking about the volunteer program in the community, and supporting the volunteers and the staff by acting as liaison between them. The volunteer program manager thus functions as administrator of the entire program, and skillful administration is crucial to success.

In keeping track of each volunteer work situation, an important ingredient is the balance between too much and not enough concern. As a volunteer program manager, you need to check regularly with each volunteer by phone or in person to find out how the volunteer is doing, how he or she feels about the work, what problems have been encountered, how relations with staff are going, and so on. You should also check with staff members who supervise volunteers to find out whether they're satisfied with the volunteers' work and whether their needs for help are being met. If problems are uncovered in this checking routine, you can then work with the volunteer and the staff person to try to resolve the situation or, failing resolution, to reassign the volunteer to another job. If the situation is working well, you can simply back off and check in again when you feel it's appropriate to do so. Asking how things are going can uncover problems before they get serious and save volunteer placements that might otherwise be lost.

Regularly scheduled monthly or bi-monthly meetings of all volunteers are a good way to provide on-going training, maintain contact with each volunteer, give volunteers a chance to help and support each other, and get information from volunteers that will help you improve the volunteer program. These meetings also tend to strengthen the ties of volunteers to the organization. As mentioned before, on-going support or training meetings should be an integral part of the volunteer job if you really want volunteers to come to them. In planning the meetings, think through your goals (on-going training, peer support, team building, evaluation of each volunteer's progress) and use a format that will allow these goals to be achieved, e.g., group discussion of issues and problems volunteers are facing on the job. Asking volunteers to help plan the meetings may add to their relevance and to the enthusiasm of the volunteers in attendance.

Keeping accurate records is another way of keeping track of your program. Provide volunteers with a way of reporting their hours to you: a sign-in sheet at the office, a monthly form for those who do their volunteer work away from the office, a phone-in system, or whatever works best for your organization. Make a monthly report to your Executive Director and/or Board of Directors of the hours volunteers have put in; it's usually an impressive record of the community support you have and, when converted to monetary value, gives a concrete figure for the contribution you receive from your volunteers. (The usual way to establish this figure is to multiply the hours by the going rate for each type of work volunteers do: minimum wage for envelope stuffers, $6.00 or so per hour for office work, $20 to $60 per hour for professional consultation, etc.)

A personal record for each volunteer is also important. You can keep a file or card on each volunteer listing length of service, changes in assignments, etc. You can also keep a ledger listing each volunteer and the number of hours he or she contributes each month. A file folder with a registration form and periodic performance evaluations can be an important record for writing references, which volunteers may ask you or your successor to do in the future. When a volunteer leaves, a final evaluation or exit interview form plus an evaluation of the program by the volunteer can be completed and included in the volunteer's file. All this record keeping may be less exciting than contact with people, but it's an important administrative aspect of the volunteer program manager's job.

Promoting your volunteer program in the community is another important aspect of the job. Getting feature articles into local papers, giving talks at clubs or church groups, and continuously publicizing your volunteer opportunities are on-going processes. Remember that a year-round public relations program is one of your best recruitment tools. You have to keep coming up with new approaches and new material in order to retain the interest of the community. Using experienced volunteers to help in this public relations effort can be very effective.

As a volunteer program manager you have two major concerns: are the needs of the organization being met, and are the needs of the volunteers being met? Since volunteers take staff time and energy, they must be giving more than they're taking or the program isn't working. In other words, the benefits to the organization's clients must be greater than the cost in staff time and incidental expenses for the organization to sustain its commitment to the volunteer program. On the other hand, volunteers won't stay unless they're getting back what they want, whether it's training, social contacts, or the feeling of being needed and appreciated. The needs of both the organization and the volunteers are of vital concern, and the volunteer program manager's role as liaison between the staff and the volunteers is a pivotal one. It's often a balancing act requiring sensitivity, understanding, and tact to keep the wheels moving smoothly.

VOLUNTEER RECORDS NEEDED

1. Volunteer hours
   a. Report form or sign-in sheet for each volunteer
   b. Monthly composite report of all volunteer hours

2. Volunteer Registration Form (in binder or file box)

3. Individual file for each volunteer
   a. Information Form
   b. Periodic evaluations
   c. Exit interview write-up
   d. Final evaluation by the volunteer

Sample
VOLUNTEER REGISTRATION FORM

Name_____

Address_____

_____

Phone_____ Birthday_____

Driver's License No._____ State_____

Volunteer Assignments:

1) _____

    Started_____ Ended_____

2) _____

    Started_____ Ended_____

3) _____

    Started_____ Ended_____

You can call me for:

    _____ Extra work   _____ Phoning

    _____ Mailings   _____ Typing

    _____ Delivering equipment to shut-ins

    _____ Driving patients to appointments

In case of emergency, call:_____

    Phone:_____

Sample
VOLUNTEER SIGN-IN SHEET

NAME_____

ASSIGNMENT_____

Date	Time In	Time Out	Total Hours

Sample
MONTHLY REPORT ON
VOLUNTEER PROGRAM*
VOLUNTEER REPORT FOR ⎯⎯⎯⎯⎯

Number of regular active volunteers:
Office⎯⎯⎯⎯⎯⎯⎯⎯⎯⎯
Phone⎯⎯⎯⎯⎯⎯⎯⎯⎯⎯
Patient care⎯⎯⎯⎯⎯⎯⎯⎯
Speakers Bureau⎯⎯⎯⎯⎯

Number of additional volunteers:
Mailing⎯⎯⎯⎯⎯⎯⎯⎯⎯
Other⎯⎯⎯⎯⎯⎯⎯⎯⎯⎯

Number of hours in office:	Current Month	Year to Date
Phone Volunteers		
Typists/general office		
Mailings		
Conferences, meetings, training (Patient Care Volunteers)		
Conferences, meetings, training (Office Volunteers)		

Speakers Bureau hours:		
Number of assignments		
Hours at assignments		
Travel time		
Preparation time		
Conferences, meetings, training		

Visits and hours for Patient Care Volunteers:

	#	Hrs.	#	Hrs.
Acute hospital				
Convalescent facility				
Home				
Providing transportation				
Phone calls				
Travel time				

*Such as a health care organization would prepare.

THE EIGHTH KEY
ADEQUATE RECOGNITION AND REWARDS

THE EIGHTH KEY: ADEQUATE RECOGNITION AND REWARDS

One of the biggest problems volunteer programs have is retention: keeping volunteers happy so they will stay on the job after they've been recruited, selected, and trained. Although recognition and rewards are not the entire answer, they can go a long way toward making a volunteer's experience satisfactory and encouraging him or her to stay with your organization.

Recognition comes in many forms, both formal and informal. Formal recognition can include pins or certificates given after designated numbers of service hours. Annual recognition dinners or parties where staff honor the volunteers also serve to thank people formally for their contributions. You can do special things: nominate one of your volunteers for a community award if there is one in your area, submit an article to the local paper about a volunteer's contribution, introduce a volunteer in your own newsletter, or give a special award to a long-time volunteer.

These formal awards are important, but two notes of caution are in order. First, events and award ceremonies can become rote and meaningless if done mechanically every year. To counteract this, get new staff members with fresh ideas involved in the planning or change the type of event you hold. Second, formal recognition only happens periodically, and volunteers need to be appreciated more frequently than once a year at the annual dinner.

That's where informal recognition comes in. A sincere "thank you" or a statement like "we missed you last week when you were on vacation" shows volunteers they are needed. Giving volunteers more responsibility, such as helping train new volunteers or speaking to a service club on behalf of the organization, provides recognition of the individual's value. You can also encourage staff to recognize volunteers by including them in staff meetings, inviting them to staff parties, or conferring with them about specific clients. As stated earlier, recognition and appreciation from the volunteer's supervisor are important, but so are recognition and appreciation from the organization as a whole. It is the responsibility of the volunteer program manager to see that volunteers get this from the organization in both formal and informal ways.

Recognition is one reward volunteers get for their work, but it isn't the only one. People are seeking a variety of rewards through their volunteer jobs, and it is part of the volunteer program manager's job to find out which rewards volunteers want and see that each gets what he or she needs. Without the reward of a paycheck, volunteers will not stay unless their motivational needs are met. (See list of possible volunteer motivations at the end of this chapter.)

You can find out these needs by the questions you ask during the interview process: why are you interested in this job, what do you want to get from this volunteer experience? Whether it's social interaction, job skills, or new experiences, the more you meet the volunteer's needs, the more likely he or she will stay on the job. Once you know why a volunteer is there, you need to make sure the volunteer's supervisor knows why as well, since the supervisor's role is crucial in giving assignments and setting work conditions. While the organization cannot pander to the volunteer, there must be a healthy balance between meeting the organization's needs and meeting the volunteer's needs for the placement to be successful.

"Adequate" recognition and reward is, therefore, relative to the individual volunteer. The more types of recognition you offer, the better the chance you will provide meaningful rewards to each person. The more you know about each person's motivation, the better the chance you will meet his or her needs and keep the volunteer on the job. Of course, volunteers will leave your organization for many reasons over which you have no control: moving away from the area, change in employment, illness, etc. However, you can improve your retention record by knowing your volunteers as individuals and providing the rewards and recognition that are appropriate to each of them.

VOLUNTEER MOTIVATION/REWARDS SOUGHT

1. Opportunity to use a particular skill.

2. Opportunity to learn or develop a particular skill.

3. Job training for future employment.

4. Opportunity to explore a possible career.

5. Opportunity to do something about a problem the individual cares about.

6. Opportunity to be part of the organization.

7. Opportunity to develop interpersonal skills.

8. Opportunity to help someone in exchange for help received.

9. Social intervention.

10. Opportunity to be part of a particular activity.

11. Desire to be involved in a "socially useful" activity.

12. Feel needed and appreciated.

13. Be recognized at a formal event.

14. Receive pin and/or certificate.

15. Get name in newsletter, newspaper, or other media.

SOME METHODS OF INFORMAL RECOGNITION

1. Saying "thank you."

2. Providing good physical surroundings.

3. Giving volunteers message boxes.

4. Letting volunteers know they are missed when absent.

5. Making sure volunteers know about new developments in the agency.

6. Inviting volunteers to participate in staff meetings, staff in-service training, and staff social events.

7. Taking volunteers to lunch or coffee.

8. Asking experienced volunteers to help train new volunteers.

9. Giving volunteers the opportunity to take on new responsibilities when they are ready.

10. Consulting with volunteers in their areas of expertise.

11. Reimbursing out-of-pocket expenses for volunteers.

12. Sending birthday cards or celebrating the volunteer's birthday with a cake at the office.

13. Paying for the volunteer to attend a training session related to his/her volunteer position.

14. Complimenting volunteers on specific things they do well.

SOME METHODS OF FORMAL RECOGNITION

1. Annual recognition dinners or parties.

2. Pins or certificates for designated hours of service.

3. Certificates of appreciation.

4. An honor roll of volunteers posted in your reception area.

5. Special awards for long-time volunteers.

6. Articles about a volunteer in newspapers or newsletters.

7. Nomination of a volunteer for a community service award.

THE NINTH KEY
SYSTEMATIC EVALUATION

THE NINTH KEY: SYSTEMATIC EVALUATION

Evaluation is an important management tool. Evaluating both individual performance and the program as a whole will point up the strengths and weaknesses of your volunteers and your program. Of course, just evaluating isn't enough; you have to act on the results of the evaluation, making necessary changes to improve performance and service.

For volunteer program management, several types of evaluation are important: 1) periodic evaluation of each volunteer's performance; 2) evaluation of the volunteers' services by clients; 3) evaluation of the volunteer program by staff; and 4) evaluation of the monetary contribution of the volunteer program to the organization's services.

There is some controversy as to whether formal performance evaluations should be done on all volunteers. Formal evaluations are an important communication tool, especially for volunteers in paraprofessional roles or those wanting to use their volunteer work for job experience. In gathering feedback from staff to write the evaluation, you learn more about both the staff person and the volunteer, and you are often able to pass on appreciative comments as well as constructive criticism. However, it is not necessary to use formal performance evaluations for jobs like periodic mailings, etc. You have to use your common sense about when evaluations are appropriate.

For the jobs you do evaluate formally, it should be done with the full knowledge and cooperation of both staff and volunteers. You should make regular evaluations a part of your written policies and let volunteers know when they come on board that you will be meeting with them after six months (or whatever interval you choose) to discuss how they're doing. You can create an evaluation form which you fill out with input from staff, then use the form as a focus of discussion. Always meet personally with each volunteer to share this form, ask for his or her reactions, talk about how things can improve, have the volunteer sign the form, and give him or her a copy while putting the original signed copy in a permanent file.

In creating the evaluation form, you will be deciding what qualities and behaviors are important for each job and for the organization as a whole. Typically important areas are reliability, promptness, relations with staff and clients, relations with other volunteers, willingness to follow policies and procedures, attendance at required meetings, sensitivity, creativity, and performance of the specific duties of the job. Since these qualities and behaviors are important in paid as well as volunteer work, evaluating them is especially important for those volunteers who are using their volunteer jobs to build experience and references for entry into the job market. Having the evaluations on file makes writing references easy for you no matter how long it's been since the volunteer worked at your organization, and these evaluations are essential for your successor(s) to be able to respond to a former volunteer's request for a reference.

Having the volunteers evaluate themselves and bring that evaluation with them to your meeting is also a good idea since it forces people to give themselves feedback before they hear it from you. This can be done by asking them to fill in the same evaluation form you use, or you can give them a different kind of form that will spark discussion of their experience and their needs (see example at the end of this chapter). Usually their perceptions of their work are similar to those of the staff who work with them, but sometimes discrepancies will point out the need for intervention in the staff/volunteer situation. Some people will be mismatched with the job or the supervisor, and you can either save or change the placement.

Evaluation meetings not only give constructive criticism to volunteers, they also make sure that volunteers receive the appreciation they deserve but often don't get. If the volunteers have done a good job, they will have concrete proof in the evaluation form. As stated before, staff sometimes forget to show appreciation to volunteers, and the evaluation process can help correct this oversight.

Volunteers should know before they start working what they will be evaluated on. The evaluation form and a copy of your policies and procedures should be part of their volunteer handbook so they know what's expected of them. Making the whole process clear and explaining why you do the evaluations should lessen any anxiety the volunteer might feel.

Now a word about what to do with performance evaluation

results. If a volunteer's work is not what it should be, you and the volunteer can come to several conclusions: the expectations of the job need changing, the volunteer simply needs to try harder, the volunteer needs a different assignment, or the volunteer should terminate his or her involvement with the organization. This latter possibility has been discussed in much recent literature under such titles as "How to Fire a Volunteer." A better term for this process could be "counseling out." If a volunteer isn't right for the job and doesn't seem appropriate for another assignment, the best thing to do is help him or her see this objectively and suggest other places or types of volunteer work that might be more suitable. When a volunteer job doesn't work out, it's no one's fault; it's simply a situation that needs to be resolved. And if, after trying various solutions, none works except the volunteer's leaving, it should be a mutual decision between you and the volunteer if at all possible.

You should give volunteers every chance before making the decision to counsel them out. Meet jointly with the volunteer's supervisor and the volunteer to see if poor performance might be caused by misunderstanding or unclear expectations. Give the volunteer more training, or set up a trial period during which the volunteer will try harder and after which you will evaluate again. Offer the volunteer another assignment if that is possible in your organization. Volunteers are an important human resource, and you don't want to let them go unless they are counterproductive to your work. But if they are, it is your job as a professional to terminate their involvement in your agency. If you have tried everything you can think of, you may simply have to say, "I'm sorry, but we cannot use your services here any longer."

Poor performance is not the only ground for termination. Another is breach of confidentiality about clients, a serious offense for staff or volunteers. Another is breach of confidentiality about donors; if donors hear that someone is talking about their gifts to the agency, they may never give again. Taking advantage of a client's vulnerability (as in the case of a volunteer counselor making sexual advances toward a client) is another ground for termination. The important thing here is to have well-thought-out and clearly stated policies that give volunteers rules to follow. Then if volunteers break those rules, you have every justification to ask them to leave.

Sometimes there are such immense public relations problems in asking a particular volunteer to leave an organization that volunteer program managers find themselves keeping someone on despite the problems that volunteer is causing. The resentment of staff and other volunteers in this kind of situation can undermine the entire volunteer program. This is one of the stickiest problems the volunteer program manager faces, especially if the volunteer is a longtime financial supporter (or the spouse of one). In such situations you and your Executive Director may have to assess the problem carefully and take the risk of asking the volunteer to leave despite the possible consequences. The responsibility for the decision is yours, but the backing of your director may be crucial in absorbing the blows that follow.

Counseling a volunteer to leave is in the best interests of both the volunteer and the organization when:

- it becomes obvious that the volunteer's performance will never be what the job requires; or
- the volunteer's presence is somehow detrimental to the work of the agency.

Be honest about the reasons why you have to ask the volunteer to leave, and always try to suggest other places where the volunteer might find more satisfying work. Even in cases where termination follows a serious breach of the rules, the volunteer can learn from the experience and can make a valuable contribution to another program.

A management tool that makes both evaluation and termination more businesslike is the volunteer contract. Some programs use contracts to spell out exactly what the responsibilities of both the volunteer and the organization are. The contract is filled out and signed by both volunteer and staff member, then reviewed in six months or so. If you use a contract, you may not need an evaluation form; you can simply update the contract with new responsibilities you and the volunteer have agreed upon. And if volunteers haven't fulfilled their part of the contract, terminating their involvement is the expected outcome.

Some volunteer jobs lend themselves to contracts and others do not, even in the same organization. Contracts seem too formal for some jobs; they may, in fact, be offensive to potential volunteers. But contracts can be very effective when the volunteer wants to use the job for work experience or when the job is a special project with specific goals and a definite termination date. Contracts make expectations of both volunteer and staff clear, but having volunteers sign contracts does not guarantee that they will carry out all the responsibilities of the job or stay in the job for the time they've committed. Contracts are a tool to be used where appropriate; they are not, as some have claimed, the solution to all your volunteer retention problems.

Evaluation of the services of the volunteers by the clients of the organization is the second aspect of our discussion. This is often done as part of a broader evaluation of the organization's entire range of services. If your organization does this (often by sending an anonymous questionnaire to clients several weeks or months after they've terminated service), you can add a few questions about how satisfactory the clients found their interactions with volunteers. Staff who are in close contact with clients can ask them about their involvement with volunteers and then report their findings to you. You yourself can call clients or meet with them (as in a school or residential treatment center situation) to get their reactions and suggestions. Through this kind of evaluation you can find out how to improve your program as well as give constructive criticism and appreciative feedback to your volunteers.

Evaluation of the program by the volunteers should also be done regularly. It's an integral part of your evaluation meetings with volunteers and can also be addressed in on-going training meetings. You can formalize evaluation by asking volunteers to answer questions on a form you've created (another form!). If you don't want to ask for periodic written reactions from volunteers, you can do so when each volunteer leaves. This final evaluation can be shared with staff and, if positive, will serve as a way of giving appreciative feedback to staff. Any negative comments can be used to make constructive suggestions for change.

Staff need to have input into volunteer program evaluation too. Besides asking for feedback on individual volunteers, you can raise issues at staff meetings, talk individually to various staff members, or tell staff you are formally evaluating the volunteer program and would like their suggestions and reactions. Usually staff have enough paperwork without filling out another form, but you can get their verbal comments and write a summary yourself. Keeping in close contact with staff who use volunteers will give you on-going knowledge of how each volunteer work situation is progressing and help you improve the effectiveness of the program from the staff's point of view.

As for evaluating the monetary contribution of the program, you need to look at the budget for your program and compare the outlay with the number of hours volunteers have served for the year multiplied by a fair hourly figure for their time. The figure you come up with is often quite impressive and, though it doesn't measure the subjective value of the program, is a good argument for spending the money to keep it going and perhaps even expand.

Evaluation is a powerful tool for assessing effectiveness and bringing about constructive change. To be worthwhile, careful evaluation must be followed by action—putting into practice those changes suggested by analysis of the results. If you do this, you will avoid obsolescence and keep the program growing. You will also inspire better performance in your volunteers, which leads to better service for your clients and more positive staff involvement with volunteers. Not evaluating your program regularly will almost inevitably lead to its downfall.

Sample
VOLUNTEER PERFORMANCE EVALUATION

Name_____ Date_____

Performance Factors	*E	S	NI	Comments
Dependability				
—Availability				
—Judgment				
—Attendance at meetings				
—Following of procedure				
—Record keeping				
Interpersonal Relations				
—Relations with clients				
—Relations with staff				
—Relations with other volunteers				
—Teamwork/cooperation				
Personal Qualities				
—Neatness				
—Insight into self and others				
—Sensitivity				
—Initiative and creativity				

*E = Exceeds Requirements   S = Satisfactory   NI = Needs Improvement

Overall _____

_____

_____

_____   _____
Volunteer   Volunteer Coordinator

Sample
VOLUNTEER AGREEMENT

Volunteer_____ Agency_____
Date_____ Job Title_____
Job Description:

Responsibilities of volunteer:
1. Fulfillment of duties and time commitment as listed in job description
2. Evaluation of supervision, training, and volunteer policy
3. Attendance at required meetings

Work hours:_____
Duration of volunteer contract_____ To be reviewed on_____

Responsibilities of agency:
1. Training and supervision
2. Personnel record
3. Future work references
4. Recommendations for further responsibilities
5. Other (explain in space below)

Supervisor(s):_____

_____
Volunteer   Volunteer Coordinator

Sample Agreement
CLIENT AIDE VOLUNTEERS

Volunteer agrees to:

1. Attend seven initial training sessions (once a week)
2. Attend monthly volunteer/social worker meetings
3. Visit client weekly
4. Call client bi-weekly
5. Make a commitment to be meaningfully involved in this program for twelve months.

Signed_____

Social Worker agrees to:

1. Meet with volunteer in person after case acceptance by volunteer to discuss case background
2. Introduce volunteer to client
3. Call or meet with volunteer on a regular basis to provide case-specific supervision
4. Provide feedback to volunteer about client progress or change
5. Attend monthly volunteer/social worker meetings

Signed_____

Date_____

Sample
CLIENT FEEDBACK
QUESTIONNAIRE

QUESTIONNAIRE ON VOLUNTEER PROGRAM

1. On the whole, was your contact with volunteers:

   __ very helpful   __ satisfactory   __ not satisfactory

2. Were the volunteer(s)' visits and phone calls:

   __ too frequent   __ just right   __ not frequent enough

3. Which of the following did you find helpful about their visits?

   _____ social contact

   _____ emotional support

   _____ errand running

   _____ household help

   _____ driving

   _____ support for family members

   _____ help with paperwork

   _____ sharing hobbies or interests

   _____ other _____

   _____

4. What other things could volunteers have done that would have been helpful?_____

   _____

   _____

5. Other suggestions or comments on the volunteer program:

   _____

   _____

   _____

Sample Volunteer Exit Evaluation

VOLUNTEER EXPERIENCE EVALUATION

1. What was your volunteer job at XYZ Agency?_____

   _____

   How long were you involved?_____

   Why did you leave?_____

2. Did you feel your volunteer work was a rewarding experience?_____

   Can you suggest anything that would have made the experience more meaningful?_____

   _____

   _____

3. Was the orientation and supervision by staff sufficient?____

   Any suggestions for improvement in these areas?_____

   _____

   _____

4. What is your overall impression of XYZ Agency?_____

   _____

   Would you consider becoming involved with XYZ again?___

   Would you like to remain on the newsletter mailing list?___

5. Additional comments or suggestions:

Name_____ Date_____

Address_____ Phone_____

THANK YOU VERY MUCH FOR YOUR HELP!

CONCLUSION: THE IMPORTANCE OF VOLUNTEER PROGRAM MANAGEMENT

The ideas and methods presented in this book are meant to be tools. Not every one will be applicable to every volunteer job or every organization, but the concepts are sound. Good job design, staff commitment, well-planned recruitment, careful screening and selection, appropriate training, good supervision by staff, appropriate surveillance, adequate recognition and rewards, and systematic evaluation **are** essential to a successful volunteer program. It is up to each volunteer program manager to decide how to apply the concept and tools to his or her own situation.

Among the qualities that are important in anyone who manages volunteers are organizational ability, flexibility, sensitivity to oneself and others, creativity, initiative, and a tolerance for ambiguity and frustration. Volunteer program managers are usually not obsessed with efficiency; people are their business, and people are not machines. Working with volunteers takes patience and the desire to place human values over material ones. That's what human service work is all about, and a good volunteer program **serves** everyone connected with it—clients, agency staff, the volunteers, and the entire community.

And that is why it's important to apply sound management tools to volunteer programs. There is always the danger that directors of volunteers will start managing for the sake of managing and forget their true goal: to manage a program that will provide beneficial human service to the organization's clients and the community. And good volunteer programs serve their volunteers as well by giving them the opportunity to be needed, to make a contribution of time and energy to meaningful work, and to grow in both technical and interpersonal skills. Only a well-managed volunteer program can deliver these outcomes on a consistent basis. Applying management techniques and professionalizing the role of the volunteer program manager do not, as some have feared, drive the human element out of volunteer work. On the contrary, they make it possible for that element to continue and grow as volunteer programs prosper.

As a volunteer program manager, you want to be an advocate of volunteerism in general, your own volunteers, and yourself as a professional worthy of the respect of other professions. You need to feel competent and confident about what you are doing in order to gain this respect. It is the author's hope that carefully analyzing the ideas in this book and then applying them in your own way to your own work situation will help you, the volunteer program management professional, gain competence and confidence in your program and your ability to manage it well.